ISBN:

0-914278-66-5

Cold Reading

# Cold Reading

Poems by
Laurence Goldstein

Copper Beech Press
Providence

Some of these poems appeared in *Agni, Boulevard, Film/Literature Quarterly, Hubbub, Indiana Review, Iowa Review, Louisville Review, Ontario Review, Poetry* ("Elderly Surfer," © 1989 by the Modern Poetry Association), *River Styx, Salmagundi, Southern Review, Tampa Review,* and *Texas Review.*

"Permissive Entry: A Sermon on Fame" was collected in *The Best American Poetry, 1995,* edited by Richard Howard.

Cover: "Culver City" (#6, 1987), by Tony Berlant. House; found-metal collage on wood with steel brads. 36x35 in.

For information, please write the publisher:
Copper Beech Press
English Department
Box 1852
Brown University
Providence, Rhode Island 02912


Library of Congress Cataloging-in-Publication Data
Goldstein, Laurence, 1943-
    Cold reading : poems / by Laurence Goldstein. — 1st ed.
        p.   cm.
    ISBN 0-914278-66-5 (alk. paper)
    I. Title.
PS3557.O396C65    1995
811'.54—dc20                                                95-3622
                                                            CIP


Set in New Baskerville by Louis Giardini
Printed and bound by McNaughton & Gunn
Manufactured in the United States of America
First Edition

This book is dedicated to
Carolyn See and John Espey,
with love and gratitude

# CONTENTS

## 1

## 2

## 3

Part I

# RITCHIE VALENS

The barrio's no garden
but it bred a California sport
hardly more Mexican than myself.
War babies came in all colors.
They made the jukebox jump, filled
the make-believe ballroom with themselves,
a culture of baby-faced Eddies
and Peggy Sues, eager to whirl
round any Ritchie, their throbbing sun.
I, too, danced his hits, hearing
the folk nonsense of *La Bamba*
as the song of that sumptuous world
across the border from rock 'n' roll.
I danced with blond angels in L. A.,
grateful not to hear Yiddish, not
live in Odessa where my pious cousins
would never tune in
the driving Bandstand of my dreams.
I was a first-stage rocket,
beginning the beguine of a strange future
no less than my brown double
who made his few immortal poems
before fame shot him from the sky.

# PRESCHOOL VISITATION

> *There is for every man some one scene, some one adventure,*
> *some one picture that is the image of his secret life, for*
> *wisdom first speaks in images.*
>
> W. B. Yeats

The troops had come home, not quite American,
more like steerage — quarrelsome refugees,
unwilling grease monkeys, flatfeet, scabs.
The Nazis lived on as invective, their camps
the everlasting site of family wrangles.
Even at three, the meaning of life struck me
as sorrowful, my Russian grandfather slapping
my left hand when I started to write or draw.
War baby, sinister only child
of a rich country recovering from a crusade.

Los Angeles had its little Israels;
we lived in one, before it changed color,
in one of many courts close to the butcher shop,
part of the fish-man's route, and vegetable-man's
and the bearded man's in black who took money
and gave it to Palestine, *where we all should go.*
I found the spot on a map. Was this my destiny,
to wrest Jerusalem from the ruthless Canaanites?
Then it was war again, and our quarters
helped feed a Joshua's army of emigrants.

These were grown-up problems, thank God.
I was five, poised to enter kindergarten,
and daily I circled the school's twisted fence,
peering beyond the foursquare and tether-ball
into rooms with wall-maps, globes, and shelves
groaning with hieroglyphs of the Golden State.
*Let me in:* the caption on this movie still.
Russia was our enemy, one boy whispered
through the rusting iron, "and there are bombs
that can blow up the whole stinking world."

So what did it matter, when an invitation
summoned me for afternoon play with a girl
who would sit next week as another stranger
in those tan desks with crayon and pencil trays,
some daughter of the next block who knew me
only by sight, that gaunt kid passing
the house, hanging on the fence like a DP?
She was Alice Obregón who wore party dresses
all the time, my mother said, a sign
of high-caste Hispanic origins.

*Something* was consequential, for I was dressed
in my seder clothes, and told some etiquette
and sent alone, a gentleman caller, to her door.
Alice came at me with a leap of animal joy,
twirling her green skirt with crimson sash.
Unsettled, I entered my first gentile residence.
Wall-hangings everywhere; no plaque of Roosevelt
or classic paintings but fabric of bizarre design
and furniture that smelled like Western movies,
pungent leather and sheepskin that made me sneeze.

Would I like some tea or café? I was a ghost
with no informal speech for this Princess
who sat us down to a china service and poured
rainbows of juice from mango and cantaloupe.
A servant set out strangely spiced cakes
dark-skinned and moist; I savored their sesame
while dolls of doeskin in lace with gold buttons
huddled with Their Lady. How beautifully
Alice's mother pronounced *Los Angeles* and
*Santa Monica,* her nasals a new music.

We were playing house, Alice and I,
wifey at the patio fountain with her mate,
the very doubles of my folks on Saturday night
dressed for nothing more than movies or prime-
rib at a swell roadhouse — and how
I felt struck by the lightning of *my* role,
chattering who-knows-what nonsense
with cosmopolitan gusto as Alice
beamed domestically at her social triumph.
Now I was two people, barely tilted

toward the shiksa bride I found in college
and the protocols outside my heritage,
half-secret like the sin of assimilation.
In the treasure house of her ancestral land
Alice made me civil, not her Cid
but no longer, quite, the yid who feared
every native type and shade of the unknown.
Why else in the Nineties would I recall
one communion among so many afternoons?

And how unlikely it is that Alice,
of whom I remember nothing more, who
I left behind after a year when
my parents crossed into Culver City,
following our kin farther west,
has summoned in thought that fugitive boy.
Yet neither of us is lost. Alice
stands in an aura beside the person she is,
a bright quetzal caged in my domain,
perpetually waiting under her roof of red tile.

# MY YEARS IN THE RESISTANCE

Like D'Artagnan, I would have led a charge
against the Cardinal's bedaggered bodyguards,
or held some gateway against Zulus or Thugees
or left home on a raft, if there had been a raft,
but to take a lighted object into my mouth,
pull the waste of burnt tobacco into my lungs
as so many friends performed in the local park
and vacant corners of the junior high —
no, I funked this burning issue of youth,
I made queasy excuses, and carried my shame
back to the supervised reading rooms,
counterrevolutionary and librarian's pet.

Only Galahad of my early teens,
I liked the style on others: parents, teachers,
authors on book jackets, Bogart and Raft
in the beat-em-up classics on Channel 9.
Only I was bereft of cool, the daunted exception
in every Saturday's good time, imagining
*some* girl out there would be too eager
to care whether a pack swelled my pocket,
and love me for my minty breath, my
encyclopedic knowledge of the American League
and Sherlock Holmes (who smoked, of course),
my sissy skill at forming lines that rhymed.

How much strength of will I had then!
Sitting in a circle of friends, and passing up
the cigarette passing like the staff of manhood.
Put a square frame over the image:
a child backing into independence,
pure-throated misfit of the Fifties, waving
my Dedalean wings against the smoke-
screen of good-digestion ads in *Life*
and the worldiness of that white talisman,

walking the boulevard with no prop,
no ready comfort, no toxic glamour,
nothing but a thin flame unto myself.

# SUBTERRANEAN

Lester, when you told me, a fellow freshman,
that emissaries from Venus parked their ships
in the hollow center of the earth, and transmitted
orders to a few visionaries like yourself,
of course I badgered you with lame jokes,
calling you "madman" till you got mad
and dissolved our friendship one day in the stacks.
What I never said, too cool to confess,
was that I, too, had once believed
in some Verneal realm of occult energy,
accessible by volcano, or mineshaft,
or high-tech archeological dig.
In the global sinkhole of my reveries
some spelunker would find a colony
of aboriginal mites, or rats, acting out
evolution's primal stages, shaping
a creaturely Eden like the lost America.

This summer I thought of our fantastic theories
as I toured the tunnels of Mammoth Cave,
descending five levels to the somber river
where blind fish drift the currents
cutting subterranean domes and grottos —
the parking lots you imagined, Lester,
the better to seek them out, and settle
among the alien race calling you from home.

Now another millennium is ending.
I hear from a friend that you inventory
titanium at Rockwell and moonlight
to raise a large family, no longer
a believer in anything but paying the bills.
I'm a skeptic, too, and yet I've stood
before twenty years of young scholars
guiding them through English underworlds,

"caverns measureless to man," the abyss
of Demogorgon and the deep-sunk domain
where Adonis learns the rites of love.
When they ask about symbols, I say
yes, the cave is a figure of the unconscious,
site and source of abundant desire.
When they ask about plausibility
I answer that everything Romantic
is credible as what a freshman sees
before childhood expires, true to life
as the invisible host we meet in cemeteries
summoning us to follow them down.

# IN MEMORY, J. T.

Blue exuberant shirts, "because
the sky is my heart's glad apparel."
"I'm an *objet d'art*," you confessed,
"and fated to increase in value."

The Sixties, Grad School of the Absurd.
Always there was a gaudy premium
on wit never meant for the page.
"Camper than Thou," our boisterous credo.

With so much flamboyant speech
your gay manner hardly stuck out;
parsing 16th-century plain-songs
was queer enough, a studied affront

to your pious housebuilding father
who bankrolled your seminars
and queried when you would alchemize
the leaden style into a paycheck of gold.

"I'm already a marked man,
stranger to my contemporaries
than Googe himself, or Gascoigne.
Tell me, who of these passers-by

would not call me fruitcake
if I recited some elegy
that moved the pre-Elizabethans
to authentic tears. Now *it's* dead,

and I'm alive, in my blue blouse,
the color of joyful disposition."
O Jim, your quicksilver phrases
lightened our discourse like grass.

You put nothing on paper, no letters,
no entries in the MLA archive,
and so the notice with your name in print,
two decades later, is a nonce item.

You're gone in the plague, not the one
rats carried into Nashe's age
but our unique erotic woe
drilled into you like the ABCs.

Do I remember right your praise
of the obscure minority, of poets
memorable for just one line,
"*Timor mortis conturbat me*"?

And your desire to titillate
some sleepy faculty, some
sub-sub-urban college town,
"my precious little purpose in life"?

And now your life is done. Donne
was "out of my field," you joked,
too antic, too far along in the '90s,
but didn't he toll for you, too?

Now you've joined the majority,
signified by a stone and a verse,
no less anonymous for rising untimely
into the homogeneous blue.

# LOST FRIEND

I hope this isn't an elegy, Tom.
Twenty years ago, Fate hooked
its blue drapery across the life we shared.
A poem is what I have instead of you —
you who would leave the room when a poem was read,
who wanted a poem-free America,
some Walden Two run by science teachers,
safe from imagination that makes our pain.

Friendships are so much like poems,
brief affinities, chance and happy
conjunctions no one can adequately explain.
In high school we were smart and talkative,
we bruited contempt for seniors going
nowhere fast, twice as fast as us:
we needed 120 credits at UCLA
before the Ivy League's third degree.

When we scampered east, you to Harvard,
me to Brown, our contact dwindled in the cold;
our wives made it more tenuous still,
mine a stewardess, yours a drifter
in love with your lockstep toward the Ph.D.
It was the late '60s; you wouldn't march
on Washington, I wouldn't admire Skinner or
your dry data-filled lab reports.
Baseball became our guarded topic, the perennial
Red Sox slump, not unlike your own
faltering progress, before the graduate school
put you on the street, a Master of Arts.

One night you rode the subway crosstown
to fetch two steaks my wife had lifted from the plane.
You called early next morning, you were
eating one of the steaks, rare, like a rat,

you said, that eats anything, any time.
Life was hard, humiliating. No, not so hard,
I said. "Yes, it is! It's fucking *hard!*"
That's the last word I had from you.
You ate the other steak. You left Cambridge.
I rubbed your name from my address book
and, one day, you did the same with mine.

# HIGH SCHOOL REUNION

Nothing has moved them to tears
more often than yearbooks, and now
they circulate table to table
keeping time with "The Great Pretender,"
theme song for this evening's masquerade:
"I seem to be what I'm not, you see."

No changing back to what they are.
Worldly fictions, they reminisce
as if their hard-won maturity
were some Circe's trick, some
stratagem only their fellow swine
can minister to by memory's charm.

It's not the Blessed Isle here
where fey lovers reunite;
no, these are still the strangers
of 1960, faces one never
kissed or punched out, bodies
one never held midnight till dawn.

> Where is the cheerleader's fabled zone,
> Her jiggling curves in the school yell?
> Where's the halfback's muscle tone,
> The grace of champions? Gone to hell.
> Where's the BMOC's pride of status?
> He's "between jobs." And the belle
> Who iced unworthies from the Saxon Princesses?
> Where is that bitch?
> > Let memory tell.

Girdled in style, they dance as if
they had the infinite luck of seventeen,
resembling as they twist and frug
what's malappropriate for middle age.

O the heart would have it otherwise!
Drink blood from this cocktail glass,

let this half-lit hall be hallways
and these same revelers approach,
one pulse-beat, now the crew-cut
and pony-tailed eidolons
ageless as the yearbook snaps
ironed on their identity cards . . .

Time's up! All protean forms
be seniors of the Nineties again!
You are not your impersonations,
not Eisenhower's happy wards.
This occasion informs against you.
Monday, none of you will be at school.

    Where are the bathroom guards?
    Have they been flushed by the bell?
    The witch who filled out detention cards,
    The Jehovah-like Vice-Principal,
    Coaches and counselors of the Establishment,
    Elders who kept us young, for a spell,
    Have they shuffled off to retirement,
    Or worse? Where *are* they?
                 Let memory tell.

# THE SILENT MOVIE THEATER

I

In my Southland were many shrines:
the Shrine Auditorium where befezzed
salesmen on climacteric binge
nodded in velvet seats, never heeded
the mumbo-jumbo of their leading men;
the Angelus Temple where Aimee Semple,
hyped Magdalene of Echo Park,
broad-cast her Foursquare Gospel
so loud and lurid even Jews tuned her in;
whatever restuccoed or whitewashed
soul-food diner new-placarded Praise God
where a preacher could shriek and
wreak his Baptist will on the unredeemed —
*there* was latter-day Mission Los Angeles.

I never forget thee, Zion, but
revisit thee all summers of my middle-age.
Fairfax, avenue of oral delights:
hot tongue on rye at Canter's deli,
poppyseed rolls tart as the spit-
and-argue aphorisms of Little Israel;
Television City, where talking heads
still bite their time, time on their side,
and Farmers' Market cries — "Kosher pickles!
Ripe cantaloupes!" — tamped in my brain for life.

Hollywood lies where seedy traffic
found and fostered it, "a kind of Athens"
or "ivory ghetto," survivors called it.
Punk shops and gay nightclubs
mark the stations west toward Fairfax
where this obsolete Theater sags,
this white irrelevant cloister
closed like an iris, the boards up,

showcases grimed where stars once beamed,
the very dirt graffitied with harsh words
Lillian Gish never put her lips around,
the two-sheets of Chaplin torn,
cashier's box sealed with masking tape.


II


Two keepers quiet as the wooden seats
took my obol, motioned me toward
the warm room of never more than twelve,
lone youth in love with antiquity,
almost a ghost myself but made American
by the dumb makeshift of archaic life.
I sat at the pitted screen, an early reader
impatient with titles, a seer no friend
would follow to that sanctuary
forty years off-road from where it's at.

In sequence, the ensemble furor of the clowns,
a naughty child's balletic tit for tat;
sea-devils dismasting galliots or brigs;
No Man's Land, a frenzied masque of boys
running pell-mell to Kingdom Come;
and most alluring, those sultry lovers
eye-locked in absolute trance.
How the old-timers of my congregation
wriggled forward, kids at nickel matinees,
watching Gilbert ogle Garbo,
Valentino inflame Banky with a glance.
In other epics, the soul was a character, too,
*Judith of Bethulia*, say, or
*Romola*, whose otherworldly sister
in her untainted habit
was ever my afterimage of angelic light.

III

Sound persuades us to be real.
Love words when lying at peace,
banter, apology, selfish command —
all speech acts leash us like pets.
In even the most automated
tentative silences of our lives
a single word sets the dial,
puts us irresistibly in sync.
And for all our sentences, death
comes due, finger to his lips,
in the midst of holiday or sex,
a period not eight decades of eloquence
will stir from its uninflected place.


IV

Twilight, August, near-gridlock
where Melrose carries Old World idioms
further east of Fairfax by channels
more fluent than Jordan or the sea.
Pick any strange kid and call him
son and heir, too late for silent film.
White shirt, black yarmulke,
pressed wool pants and laced-up shoes;
at a synagogue door he pauses,
stayed by the Scriptures' demands
or a street cry — "Jesus, look out!" —

leans forward, and exits on a wipe

enters a house of cedar and fir
carved with open flowers and palms.
The Torah unrolls its white expanse,

its mute backward recitative —
characters more fatal than nitrate's
even now expiring as you read.
Hieroglyphs must have interpreters;
mine were the mute Davids and Delilahs
in the ruined warehouse of visual aids.
All those apparitions from 1925,
those cartoons of the passionate life,
I summon here for this pre-bar-mitzvah boy.

Those moving murals of Jerusalem
were blessed — this I believe — and
no less if Talkies outlived them.
Some day it happens, a new testimony:
"How now brown cow" spoken into a mike;
wired for radio, a Jew sings "Mammy,"
tells my teenage parents, "You ain't heard nothin' yet."
On me, too, the stylus of movie prattle
has incised whatever speech I share;
more actor than author, I playback
phrases in circulation on screen and off.
I wish *these* words, helpless if well-meant,
could make my dreamstore flicker again;
once a week its grand period pantomimes
graced a city clamorous to be loved;
now they have closed their destinies,
*Kol Nidre* come upon their last temple,
a ruthless repossession, like the Lord's.

Part II

# ELDERLY SURFER

No more cold creeps for you,
old man, leathery outlier so long
steeped before dawn in the numbing
Pacific rhythms of swell upon swell,
the *I am/iamb* of rising to the board
and shooting the curl, skiing
that steep face inimical to man,
and then just short of shore-break
turning your back on the furry
beach towels and bedroom eyes
of Laguna girls, the empty
lifeguard station, to paddle again
two whale-lengths further than
any teen pretender dares, and wait;
what is time but a quicker take-off,
a smoother passage through the tube,
a hundred-thousand cycles of the sea-god's
vehement charity, even now flexing
and rolling toward you
the radiant thunder of a perfect wave?

# SUMMER CAMP FUND

Even she is tired of saying, "The novelty is gone"
and hearing others say, "You never looked so good."

   *Stephanie needs to increase her involvement opportunities*

Sometimes she watches TV movies about people like herself.
Now she is reading another book about people like herself,
whose ancestors came to America with a dream,
who shop on Rodeo Drive and drive a Jaguar
and speak the languorous argot of the tailor-made.

   *Won't you help her to a change of scene?*
   *She needs to know there's another life out there*

Once she was attracted to a picture of the desert,
in an ad about transient lifestyles for the 1990s.
It showed a black model and a lot of sagebrush
and nothing behind her but a yellow pool of earth.
She shopped for days before she found a match.

   *Her peer interaction has steadily decreased*

"It's not safe to live in this city anymore."
"It's getting so you're afraid to leave the house."
"The traffic is terrible! Why can't all these people stay
      where they were born!"
Yolanda overhears these sentences, says nothing but
"La comida, señora," three times a day.

   *She needs positive interaction in a non-alienating space*

The camp is in the desert. Or in the mountains.
There are no locks on the doors. There are no doors.
The Others are hand-picked, the animals are wild.
At night there is nothing to do, nothing, except

watch the moon alter its shape, growing
like the memory of a full life, then waning,
then growing, then waning.

*Please open your hearts and your checkbooks*
*Please expand Stephanie's horizons before it's too late*

# GIRL AT A SCHOOL FOR THE EMOTIONALLY DISTURBED

You're not homeless; indeed, this hospice
of the congenial world, this mountain aerie
funded by the guilty, well-meaning rich
boards you in splendor no ghetto kid,
no middle-class, has known except in films.
You pay back the Fates by cooking broccoli,
serving your abnormally sweet-tempered class.
The regimen consoles you, like botany,
the curricular center, the locus of orderly life
on the California part of the planet you call home.

Once promiscuous, wanting someone's touch
or wanting the costly blow of hit after hit,
now you take comfort from the pledge "No sex,"
free to share a shawl in the Sierra chill,
unsupervised, with the boy who suffered
genital abuse and took some moly of affluence,
little seeds, to evacuate bad dreams.
Sexuality can skip a generation,
the family survives, Rosacae, in full bloom
ready to fill niches like the fingers of dawn.

You work hard, for a change, not only scrubbing
but asking the hard questions of your peers
as they probe you for the dirtiest version —
"No euphemisms" — of the hell you enjoyed.
Though none wears black, color of wild parties,
and wall-hangings are prescriptively gay,
what you say is uglier than what Plath
uttered in Esther's tale; no wonder *this* estate,
safe from parents, dry, drug-free and fenced,
gleams with polish like the blue around the clouds.

Three otherworldly years, and then
the rickety bus with its exotic plants
maneuvers downhill on the tense curves
and stops, too soon, in the city with a Spanish name.
The terminal is full of strangers, and the train
carries more tumbleweed like yourself.
How many uprootings, fugitive teen, and
how many asylums will nurture you
before that furtive smile you hazard to men
crosses your plot like a witch's charm?

# IS REALITY ONE OR MANY?

No one would put it that way
anymore, as young Socrates did
and then endured Parmenides'
pontifical demonstration;
the more modern query is this,
from my eight-year-old son:
"Can a second baseman also
play left field? And who decides?"
The manager decides, I say,
taking the easy question first.
"Why? Can't he decide himself?"
I translate into Platonese:
Is every portion of a manifold
indefinitely numerous, or a unit?
And why is One set over Many
in this Republic more people
aspire to than occupy?

It's true, some play only one base,
one field — if well, they endure,
perhaps appreciate into All-Stars;
if badly, they are retracted
into one of us, the spectators
who may indulge in pickup games
or night-league shadow play
mimicking the true forms of the Leagues
but who are as much unlike
as like, for (Parmenides explains)
sameness and unity are different ideas.
A father is also a son, for example,
but not ever the son he wants to be,
the ideal son of his favorite myth,
nor his own son, in whose life
he participates with new-fledged hope.

By this time the boy slugger has fled.
I'm engaging myself in dialogue,
remembering how Parmenides proved
the One is in process of becoming
older and younger than itself,
like the whole ongoing law
and golden chronicles of the Leagues,
their sequence of rookies and veterans.
Baseball is One and Many at once,
offering all aspects of duration:
the diamond's luster cannot fade.

Hence happiness for my son,
not sinister as I was, conditioned
by weight and dexterity to first base,
trapper-mitt my sign of difference,
perishing *qua* professional in
the leaden echelons of the Pony League,
but one who throws with rectitude
and swings an outfielder's bat.
Another century will measure his powers.
What though my chance of glory has passed,
I am still his fellow amateur,
neither identical nor different,
having as we do a family resemblance
no less than Dodger with Dodger,
Twin with Twin, Free Agent with
some legend from the Hall of Fame.

There, our Symposium is finished.
The twilight gives us time
for some catch, a few innings
of the Tigers on live TV,
a bedtime story about the immortal Babe.

# PERMISSIVE ENTRY: A SERMON ON FAME

Life is porous enough
for any number of interventions:
a directory's worth of neighbors,
sales personnel, colleagues disputing
*Endymion* or *Wonderland*, the sexpot on Channel 2;
at the margins of consciousness
the junk-mail, or noise, of
infinite presences grind their unrecorded
deeds, as if mere activity mattered.

One can grant them valuable life
they hardly deserve, like Bernstein
in *Citizen Kane* who lets a pretty passer-by
haunt his autumnal reveries; she's
the softer spirit he sacrificed to Kane.
Bernstein or Goldstein, Mankiewicz or Welles,
who hasn't, if only from perversity, kept
some indulgent memory of a rose-lipped beauty,
a face for the lost happiness of life?

Biographies seldom tell us this. Letters
may do so: candid, egocentric, shameless,
they reveal the poet in August 1945 worried
exclusively about an acquaintance's sour review
in a Cleveland daily, how the McCarthy terror
went unnoticed by an actress who fumed at extras
or daydreamed of an admiral. Decades afterward
we circulate to flesh and blood over a fine dessert
the contagious novelty of such dated gossip.

It's more than the wary glance at the watering hole;
some arbitrary fame we envy, and cherish,
the incidental unearned influence
that outlasts a mother's devotion, as a bon mot
may be all we remember of a friendship.

Blame it on timepieces, masscom, aging,
this reflex salute to some Bulkington,
nothing more than a shape washed overboard
to float, but never quite sink, in the circumambient flood.

Like the South African who chattered
one July evening in 1961, on a crowded cargo boat
plying between Brindisi and Haifa, planning
his post-adolescent return to Johannesburg
after seven years of sowing wild oats.
"That's an awful place," one heckler said,
and he rejoined, "We're all traveling to our separate hells."
Whoever he is, and wherever, he would never believe
how often his overheard remark has braced me in solitude.

The vitality of chance utterance
is reason enough for art, a mirror & medium of
permissive entry into the universe of lives.
Like Thoreau, we occasionally lop off
fluent humanity and "center" ourselves, grow bored,
set off on the Concord, inviting strangers
to "impact" upon us, and write them briefly down.
Each is an imaginable subject,
a minor note in the swelling music of ourselves.

Some in every generation
obsess all contemporaries; others must settle for less,
celebrities only to a few. So what? Enough to
impinge like . . . there! . . . two terriers capering by,
performing our walk-ons for no special audience,
while summoning to alert attention
now and tomorrow, the Elect our wistful voices
strain at, less and less audibly, echoes
of all castaways gone into the deep.

# BEST-SELLING AUTHOR

Are you a better dreamer than I am,
goldenhair twisted and teased, your
smart tongue writhing like an adder?
On talk shows you rhapsodize
how tome after tome you transfer
some shop-keeping Jewish couple
from shtetl to Ghetto of Opportunity,
and three generations later
an offspring queens it in Hollywood,
coiling her rare fur at the camera . . .
It's you, princess! that self-made
heartthrob with sugar for brains.
You format the family history,
shaping for the Old-World-at-heart
happy endings sauced with lies.

At Thrifty Drug, my starstruck mother
buys these palliatives off the rack,
talks them up like a shill
who stops passers-by in the casino
and flatters the slots' abundance,
the Twenty-One tables' unbelievable largesse.

"Mama, if I broke the bank, still
it wouldn't be enough." If I said that,
she would answer in a TV sort of voice,
"Then what are you doing here, honey,
in this desert watering hole,
betting your savings on baccarat?"

# I DOUBLED FOR ORSON WELLES

*For the first time in his life he began to feel a loss of identity.*
*Due to reasons that he did not quite understand . . . a number*
*of people began to address him as Orson.*
                    F. Scott Fitzgerald, "Pat Hobby and Orson Welles"


My creator, the boy wonder
who penned *This Side of Paradise*
so young it brings sappy tears
to my old jaundiced eyes . . .
at least he never lived to see
how Orson outsmarted himself,
watch Hollywood's toughest ham
mug his way through fluff
even I could have improved.
Like me, he idled "between pictures"
most of his posthumous career,
like my author, too, shoring up
self-respect a whole decade
with my adventures, or worse,
while glamorizing Kid Thalberg
for his boffo comeback role.
Previews of fading attraction — that's us,
my maker patching me into
the continuity of the golden age
like the "good man for structure" he was.

I was good enough to survive
thanks to benzedrine and the races,
good enough to pass, once,
for an American original —
but that insert was a lousy joke
Scott made at my expense,
one of his many jokes on me
who all during deathwatch at the morgue
kept sober reciting his sentences
and touched his wrinkled hands

in the Wordsworth Room, waiting
for the next take or process shot
to lift this ungreyed extra
like Dracula out of his sleep.
He was put to bed with a shovel
and I lived half a century on.

If living is what it was.
The studio gates forever shut,
I drowned my sorrow in The Retake Room,
sponging from East Coast literati
with memoirs of my great original.
I made a pitch to young Orson
but he had his own *Gatsby* in the can —
a swell picture it was, too —
and rollercoastered out of sight.
Do you need to hear the rest?
A script so full of coincidence,
pathos, bravado, double-cross —
a hack job credits to credits.
And those young squirt producers!
buttered and served up by the *Times*
as saviors of the industry,
those overdressed callboys
led him such a dog's life . . .
Once after some goofy rushes of
*The VIPS* we talked of Scott;
I said, "The poor son of a bitch."
Orson gazed off, soul-searching,
and said, "The poor son of a bitch."

Hollywood made and unmade me.
I learned my craft from *The Great
Train Robbery*, and I've seen all
the classics down to *F for Fake* —

my heart broke during that flick!
"It's about *you*," I told Orson
at a watering hole on Sunset.
"They're all about me," he intoned.
"What happened to heroes?" I shot back.
"Show me a hero," he smiled hugely,
"and I'll write you a tragedy."
I could never film the story I lived;
Orson did, writing behind me,
and that gave us cheer to the end.
No, I didn't visit his corpse;
I was afraid, if I tottered in,
swollen so fat myself on medication,
muffed and gnarled with disappointments,
I might shock the souvenir hunters —
like a scene I once wrote for the B's,
the living dead lurching into view,
the bit players flailing their arms,
gasping out a ghostly name —
"Orson," they'd cry, "Orson. Orson!"

# COLD READING

She has Mediterranean features,
a baggy pullover and grey skirt.
Walking on eggshells, she bows
her pageboy toward the Morris chair,
curls catlike into a corner of it.
Don't notice me, she signals
at first, but her violet eyes
bear down when I lean close.
She gives me hard cash to say
how many hungers she really is.
Cold reading, it's called, this
precarious game I make my living at.
I ask her sun sign. Libra, of course.
"Where do I live?" she challenges.
I close my eyes but peer through.
*I see apartments on a busy street* —
she frowns — *You considered them once* —
"Yes" — *but chose a modest room* —
"Yes," bitterly. *You must share
a place in that neighborhood you detest.
I see an open suitcase* — a hit!
"I'm ready any time, it's worse than home."

To follow up, I move a castle:
*You nearly died as a child.*
"He didn't think I was a child,"
she hisses and wrinkles her lips.
Now it's child's play. *Don't think
your father has no remorse.*
"Has?" *I see his specter beside you.*
She winces, raises a shielding hand:
"If daddy is here . . . Leave me alone!"
*He's gone, you've beaten him* —
yes, her look confirms it — *as once
he beat the sinner out of you.*

44

Type three she is. I tell her
about her dead-end jobs, men
who mistreat and abandon her,
how she's developed a technique
both come-on and rebuff,
easily seen through, as she intends.
*You're tense, wary, reserved inside*
*even when sociable, as now,*
*so often the most well-liked*
*of all your friends.* How she yearns
to believe that, and swallows it down.
She wants an illusion of uniqueness
and wants to melt into the crowd.
"I join the clubs and committees, but
so often I babble like an airhead.
It must be I don't really respect
those men, try too hard to please."
*Notice how sensibly and fluently*
*you speak now.* "It's because you . . . "
*You wonder, when will fortune smile —*
she's nodding — *when will your prince come?*
*Let's consult the sybilline cards.*

Now I give her a more active role.
Clairvoyant herself, she touches
the Greater Trumps and makes them speak.
Of the Moon and the World she is eloquent,
so I put them at the center of a cross,
and we conjure from the Lesser Arcana
the Ace of Hearts version of happiness.
All readings are plausible; she
takes the bad news with the good,
fingers the wounds of personality
as I reopen them by horoscope.
Credulous? Yes, when the normal fails

the paranormal must intervene
and render its reliable mercies.
(Who has needed them more than I?)
She's a classic of her type, yet
not without edges, eccentricities.
I don't settle for one-size-fits-all
divinations, once I get some facts.
Just ask my clients if I read them
with second-sight. I *am* psychic,
ever since boyhood more sensitive
to godsends, hints, and clues.
I translate according to my powers;
no guest of mine goes off unchanged.
"What sort of man will want me,
forever?" *One who understands you.*
"As you do? Aren't we yin and yang,
my stories, your intuitions?"
*You will find many like me, not*
*practitioners of the mystic art,*
*merely the admirers you will know*
*better how to attract.* "How?"
*By acting more authentically*
*what you are.* "But what am I?"
O self-willed Scheherazade,
more than I know how to command.

And now the last quarter hour.
Her past an open book, her fate
a matter of arbitration, she and I
negotiate with the cards and stars.
"Give me your power. Make me
more like what you know is best in me."
*It will grow on the nourishment*
*of your desire and my devotion.*
*My hermetic spirits truly love*

*your candor, and how your confusion*
*never mystifies more than an hour.*
"Your feelings are the same as mine, then!"
There it is. Every client
speaks in the possessive, to steal
my singularity for a fee.
*I am of you, a second father,*
*but our pure affection is privileged,*
*not the vulgar identity of mates.*
*I am your recourse, you my resource.*
"You are my familiar, and not the first.
I have more spunk than you imagine,
so many words ready to be heard . . ."
*You must offer me more words —*
*next time, a near future for us both.*

We're finished. She lingers, as if
some acute remark is in the offing,
extends her delicate hand; I study
the long palm and long fingers,
touch the mount of Venus under her thumb.
She leaves with one irritable glance.
What indirections will she dream up
to keep me guessing at her expense?
Idly, I turn over the cards:
cups, coins, swords, and wands.
I shuffle the orderly schemes
of destiny, lay out one sequence
after another, till summoned by the bell.

Part III

# IMAGING

I, too, have read too many poems
about photographs, sensitive lyrics
evoking the unworldly radiance
of the recent past: child's play, first
husband or second lover, and of course
mom and dad at the author's present age.
Please, let's have no more epiphanies.
Let's rub out the spots of time; one smear of
elbow grease obscures all windows
into the all-absorbing goaf of *temps perdu.*

I hear your response: "OK, Dr. No,
what've you got that's better?" Better
than reality, you mean, because the (w)hole
of life is all there is to subject about. . .?
You're waiting for my contra-Proust, my heresy
fomented from distaste for a genre and,
you guessed it, for my own nostalgia,
ready to blitz not only the photo-poem
but the cloudy retrospect, the humid reverie
even when smart enough to make light of itself.

I have in mind a runic mode less fixated,
neither mourning a picture nor enraged
by recollection, nor bound to visual cues
like fast-food franchises that cannot
undertake a change in the least French fry.
Experience builds selfhood, brick by brick.
Poetry is the sledgehammer to all that solid craft:
whimsy light as a rose-petal, or feints
and jabs against the tar-baby of the ego,
trashing time's clumsy kodachromes.

Don't photographs lie? The ones we save
tell only our public, permissible stories;
our genuine life is unrecorded, isn't it?
As electronic imaging renders *all*
photos suspect, the familiar photo-poem
must be digitized by Imagination's fingers
into dreamwork mused and strange, original,
memory of the present driven not by need,
not only by traumas of spurned affection
but by the glossing, laser composite of art.

Poetry makes no measly claim to the truth,
never lets the prescriptive snapshot
box our wily invention an eternity's length.
So let's hear it for the unbuttoned lay,
barbaric or ultra-civilized, but loosed
like a Dadaist in the archives, gluing
real and unreal into that unique disorder
more capacious than a romantic heaven,
current as the bright idea just beyond
the tyrannical finder of the camera eye.

# SIGNAL HILL

*in memory of Raymond Chandler*

Once the crest is reached
where a military academy
breaches the short drop
into scary neighborhoods —
bars expressing their bored
black unemployed who drift
like blood cells to the shore,
markets boarded and overwritten
with messages that pain the eye,
thrift shops, revival halls —
then the case comes to mind,
fills it like the cemetery's
unwanted dead pushing at the fence.

Ron Settles, football star
the police strung up in his cell
with the lie of suicide —
he had chased other fame,
imagined columns of praise
lighting his heraldic strides
into a color-blind Jerusalem.
Dumb jock who didn't know
the city knows the order it wants:
money in the right white pockets,
dead coyotes, tigerish cadets,
the reeking wells ravished for good.

The writer who knew it best
worked in its weed-ridden fields.
His bad cops are its pillars;
his loathsome murders come back,
keep meeting under the tongue.
*Just an accident,* they say, just

what happens in a town on the move.
Now the president complains
the air is too clean, too clear;
the acrid message fumes in the sky:
*Break somebody's head! It's okay.*
Squad cars flash red lights
down these mean streets;
shadows step back into shadows.

# FOLKESTONE, 1917

Catastrophe has its sacred history, too.
Sites where shoppers lay down,
never to garden or banquet again,
never hear anything after the splintering beams
and the *wong-wong* of Gothas in the sky.
Next month London would be the news,
the capital's alarm licking at papier-mâché
houses of sanity: Wells, Woolf, Bennett,
and the teletypes of hysterical fiction ever after.

Burning, burning. We know that story.
But there are images from Kent as well:
a conservatory's glass blown across a road
"like a thin coating of ice on a winter's day";
a draper's goods gracing the rubble,
his headless customer in a dummy's crouch;
a flower basket jammed into a picket fence.
Unapocalyptic, these ninety-five deaths
so swiftly buried by
the photogenic millions Underground
weeping their prologue to the Book of Terror.

Put down today's paper. What you have read
is an aftertype of Folkestone,
post-airship, pre-B-17,
small cicatrix nations can tear open
by a whispered word, a finger
feeling its way to a button's tip.

# LONDON

In Piccadilly, three punkers sang
"At the 'Op," flaunting flax mohawks
and tight-trousered butts, all
sloe-minded as the druggers nodding in time.

Hardly civil, these children of Eros,
nor mine who gagged on plaice & chips,
fled the vile pastries and black
puddings, unsavory English fare.

Too, we stopped reading the *Times*
that boarded its Fleet Street shop
and thundered from suburbs at drifters
cadging tenpence under Palace walls.

Palace. Abbey. Temple. Court.
The *Guardian* tried to keep secrets
but venality and class dolor
staled in code between the lines.

O City, though you hoard history,
gorge on the Devon cream of it,
chew in stalls on pentameter
stringent as fall rain to the tongue,

cavities persist, darken, throb.
No tourist should bad-mouth
or mimic in verse the uglier sounds
Sid Vicious ever spat out,

but this American cousin, kissing
in memory all features to his taste
still, ungrateful, one of Paine's
dyspeptics, makes this foul return.

# THRIFT SHOP, YPSILANTI

There he goes, my eight-year-old
second self, down the aisles
of Collectors Corner, time warp
where Sputnik and UFO replicas,
Elvis albums, worn copies of
*Peyton Place, A Summer Place,*
model Thunderbirds — all the
regalia and impedimenta
of my second decade lie in state.
I finger some wasted velvet
and summon heartache, thinking
how my old gang of boppers
divested their bodies and souls
of all this funky energy
and filled their parents' shoes —
the ones that two-step at reunions,
first and second weddings.

And here he comes with a friend,
thin-boned, perhaps Vietnamese,
whose meticulous grown-ups
test a vanity for flaws,
the father pushing his weight,
the mother maneuvering a drawer.
Already they've gathered in one drift
a hamper, a pot, and six chairs.
Their eyes hook mine; I smile down
where our boys strut with toy swords,
then look up; no smiles return,
only the unalarmed stare
of natives new to this place.

It's true, I have no business here,
no need to shop secondhand.
I kill time doing what my

second-generation mother did,
doting on novelties from the past —
a keychain, a commemorative plate,
any drinking glass adorned
with Marilyn or an astronaut.
It's not Yiddish I speak, or
the *Kol Nidre* of Cantor Rosenblatt
I seek, but some gentlest pang
appliquéd on mementoes run to camp.

My son can't talk, then won't
with his mute fellow citizen.
*I tried*, he shrugs, pulls my sleeve.
Finally I buy nothing, not
the clock with a Dumbo face,
the G. I. Joe paraphernalia,
the pennant from Niagara Falls.
None would fill the empty space
I've kept at home, the blank occasion
to hunt and hoard American goods.
Now the others begin to laugh.
Their skinny boy is playing monster;
he wears a Frankenstein mask
which they fondle, then discard.

# THE SPORTS COMPLEX

They sweat and stretch in pain; they push weighted levers
and wrestle rubber knobs right or left, and, always
on the perimeter, runners in shorts circle a track.
This is the Straining House. But will perpetual effort
do more than harden and swell muscles, including the heart?
Will charity increase with ease of breath, or poetry
be more cherished for the pull-lift rhythm of bars
or the kinetic frenzy of cycling and climbing of moving stairs?

Here for basketball, I think of Pindar, who praised
the exertion of force on the wrestling mat or the boxer's blow
that makes a name immortal for crushing a jaw. Nikeus,
I'll cite you at random to show how well the system works.
But these athletes will not live in verse, they toil
for other gain than first place in the Complex intramurals
or the now-reprehended wolf-whistle of the thoroughfares.

Better so. Who would be Ajax as the Greeks remembered him?
He earned Achilles' fancy armor by his brute strength,
a tiger who beat the Trojans down but had no defense
when the sly generals Agamemnon and Menelaus
took the spoils for themselves, and gray-eyed Athena
spread her net for the hapless hunk: he murdered cattle
in his madness, thinking them Greeks, and when sanity returned
he sharpened his bloody sword, propped it in the ground
and ran it through a body no warrior could overwhelm.

I ask myself for a moral as I choose a ball, dribble
into the key and jump-shoot. No muscle comes of this;
more likely muscle damage as I leap and fall on tendons
weak enough to feel the shock. I have a backbone
so brittle in my forties I am warned away from bodysurfing,
my teenage skill. (Even Magic pulled hamstrings
for all the practice and craft of his everyday play.)
Shooting keeps me limber, like these fey bodybuilders,

ready and able to spring forward in choral speech.
"It's a hard thing," we say in Sophocles' tragedy of Ajax,
"that we must range and plod, with never a fair course
to bring us near our goal." Unless ranging and plodding
*is* the goal, the incessant untrophied training till death.

Ball or no ball, we are goal-tending in our unremitting
half-measures of satisfaction, made a little tauter
and faster by exercise, annealed and better kneaded
into a shape and speed more acceptable to the gods.
Let's push that bar, then, pump iron, as if Pindar
declared our vain and strenuous drill praiseworthy
and inscribed our American names in the temple of fame.
Imaginary victors, we wrap our tarnished selves
with the breastplate of the hero Achilles, and deadlift
the shield fashioned in the underworld for one Fate loved enough
to make of his funeral games the graceful culture of sport.

# THE TURBULENT GOLDSTEIN PROBLEM

*Lecture: R. Melnik, "The Turbulent Goldstein Problem." 4 p.m. 107 Aerospace Engineering Building.*
                    University Record

Many problems don't have names;
like spooks or sonic booms they visit
too intermittently to wear the gravity
of nomenclature. Sudden twinges and frets —
a shot of whiskey melts them,
they flow back to the sour pool
on which our ego floats, ever-replenishing
Noah's Ark of thwarted desires.

But you know natural science: it puts
a title on the chemical kite-tail
clinging to atoms forming the molecule;
it coins a word for the safe pivot
a rocket motor can turn upon;
it latinizes the Creation, filling
encyclopedias with terms no lay
person can pronounce: echiuroid, ovoviviparity.

Now it has discovered the process
by which I vex my acquaintance, trashing
their well-meant words with misconstruals,
turning like a dynamo
their tepid bitching into operatic wars.
How I assign failing grades, nag my kids,
overfertilize the flower beds, and worse
will be verified, now I'm a fundable Problem.

From my perspective the problem is
calling myself a Problem. I cope
better than most creatures on this globe,
not always at their expense. My mug's

never hung on a post office wall.
I blow some weather into every calm,
goose a few quiescent spirits
who lead lives more customary even than mine.

Don't confuse me with my demon namesake,
the butcher of Hebron; that fury you hear
is my hammering out schemes of armistice.
I have a surefire plan for Northern Ireland,
and one to save the street waifs of Rio.
I'll leave tomorrow on a whirlwind tour
of any hotspot, if any statesman
thinks I'd be part of the solution.

Even so, I'm fated to remain a problem
to myself, and, let's face it, others.
I'll make demands till the day I die.
I'll fail in mind and body, and maybe
I'll end my days as I began, a simpleton,
some Skimpole breezing through life
like an unguided missile, a fey turmoil
not even social scientists can rationalize.

Now that I'm a declared public nuisance,
my unruliness a certified topic
no self-pity can mollify
or confession heal, why shouldn't I agitate?
I'll double my workload, roil *fortemente*,
raising Cain as best I'm able.
Aerospace will be the least of my freebooting.
O give me years to hector the world!

It's war between us, you savants
who fix the stigma of Problem on our souls.
I'll shout down your self-interested proofs,

hear no labels that chafe or constrain.
Try to make me a household word!
I'll say my inspired piece, thank you,
and go on like an eccentric twister
farmers yarn about in their dotage.